21 Days of Abundance Affirmations

Change Your Life by What You Say

By Adrienne G. Earls

SIGNATURE
—MONEY SYSTEMS LLC—

ISBN: 978-1-7343050-0-5
Unless otherwise noted, all Scripture quotations are from the King James
Version of the Bible.

Dedication

To my family: The Earls quartet!

Mom and dad, thank you for giving me life. I know I came along a little sooner than planned, but I am so glad to be here. You are the greatest parents in the world. You made sacrifices for Regina and me all your lives. We've remained close and full of love over the years. Your encouragement and expectations are the push to my drive. Mom, you are the example of a true lady and wife. Dad, you are my example of how a Godly man should live as a protector and provider for his family. I am blessed beyond measure to be your daughter.

Regina, I am proud to be your sister. We both have our ways, but we make it work in the same household. Your talents of speaking, baking and meeting planning need to be uncovered and released to the world. I know you had my back throughout this project. Thanks for believing in me!

Family members, church members, spiritual advisors and friends, my life is richer because of each of you. It is not by chance that we crossed paths. Keep the faith, keep believing and never give up! I am a witness that the prayers of the righteous produce much.

I acknowledge Jesus Christ as my personal Savior and God as my Father and Lord over my life. I owe Him everything and no matter what, God is good!

Encouragement

To the women and men who believe that abundance is your birthright, and are willing to speak it into existence, let the Words of your mouth speak truth and life. Be encouraged. Create your abundant life with the simple Words of this book. Open your hearts and minds and let the Word minister to you as never before. Hope and abundance are already yours, all you have to do is prophesy. God is ready to bless your whole life starting today.

Be forgiven.

Be changed.

Be free.

Be healed.

Be renewed.

Be restored.

Be blessed.

Be prosperous.

And be of the righteous.

Table of Contents

Introduction

Beloved,

The action on the cross of Calvary has proclaimed and certified that victory has been won. Defeat has been pushed far away from you. Health and prosperity are now yours. If you want to walk in success, you absolutely can immediately.

You have in your hands keys to taking authority over lack and poverty, by putting your eyes on Jesus instead of yourself. Ephesians 1:17-21 (AMP) tells us,

17 [I always pray] that the God of our Lord Jesus Christ, the Father of glory, may grant you a spirit of wisdom and of revelation [that gives you a deep and personal and intimate insight] into the true knowledge of Him [for we know the Father through the Son]. 18 And [I pray] that the eyes of your heart [the very center and core of your being] may be enlightened [flooded with light by the Holy Spirit], so that you will know and cherish the hope [the divine guarantee, the confident expectation] to which He has called you, the riches of His glorious inheritance in the saints (God's people), 19 and [so that you will begin to know] what the immeasurable and unlimited and surpassing greatness of His [active, spiritual] power is in us who believe. These are in accordance with the working of His mighty strength 20 which He produced in Christ when He raised Him from the dead and seated Him at His own right hand in the heavenly places, 21 far above all rule and authority and power and dominion [whether angelic or human], and [far above] every name that is named [above every title that can be conferred], not only in this age and world but also in the one to come.

Once we accept the true Word of God and who we are in Christ Jesus, we can possess the full provisions and authority of our lives. The way has been provided, and Kingdom principles and laws have been established. Godly laws which no one can alter, are firmly in place. Prosperity, wealth, riches and stewardship are terms from the Bible. This is not a new philosophy or idea, nor is this a promotion of the "prosperity gospel." This is a "re-presentation" of God's Word, for those with an ear to hear.

The spoken word has always had the power to change lives, it is also creative and will draw what you say into existence. Because it is a proclamation, one has to be careful repeating incorrect or bad reports about oneself. What you say is what you feed on and what you feed on is what is magnified and grows. Therefore, you should always say what God says about you. Come into agreement with what only He says and start confessing it.

If you are shackled or struggling with your finances, this book will help renew, restructure and return your mind to a perfect path; God's path. We were never meant to be in lack or live in poverty because we are sons and daughters of Almighty God. We are to be fruitful, multiply and subdue this earth period.

While reading this book, many have seen breakthroughs during the first 21 days, and some experience changes after day 21. I encourage you to read and recite each page with hope, boldness and expectation. Truly believe what you are saying or continue saying it until you believe. God hears you and will respond to His Word. If you are sincere and seek to unleash the benefits of our Lord, then you will see it come to pass. He is able!

Change your life by what you say.

Behold, I am thy Lord, the God of all flesh: is there anything too hard for me?

Jeremiah 32:27

Instructions

I have found that the most effective way to renew your mind is through repetition and focus. Over the next 21 days, I suggest the following steps for the 21 Abundance Affirmations to be most effective:

1.   Get a clear picture of where you desire to increase and come into agreement with God about it. Determine the financial blessings you desire and why you want them and emphasize what purpose the financial blessings will serve. We serve a big God who meets the bigger needs of His children. WE ARE BLESSED TO BE A BLESSING of hope, love and confirmation of God's covenant to our ancestors. Decide who you will bless with your abundant blessings that God Almighty has prescribed for you and began to actively pray for that person or cause.

2.   Repeat aloud all 21 Abundance Affirmations at least twice a day (the more the better, morning is best), repeating three times a day is ideal.

3.   Discontinue saying anything negative about your finances or future, dispel any form of negativity. If something slips out verbally that is not according to God's Word, repent immediately and confess what God says over the matter.

4.   Each morning, find a quiet place to read aloud that day's devotional of one of the abundance affirmations until all 21 devotionals have been completed in 21 days. Meditate on the scriptures provided for that day, even reading in different translations to get the full meaning of God's Word.

5.   Recite the morning prayer each morning and the evening prayer each evening, believing what you pray is answered when you pray. These prayers may be personalized to meet your particular needs.

6.   In a spirit of gratitude, be alert and help others in need of assistance on a daily basis. (not just limited to finances) Give any form of help and it shall be given unto you in a good measure.

7.   Practice what you are affirming and believing and press into what you are declaring over your life.   You will be speaking things that do not exist into existence. Hold fast to what you are saying. Even if you don't see them manifest right away, do not speak against them.

8.   Expect your mindset to shift, let your mindset become positively-oriented. Be grateful when your mindset has changed for the better. This is only the beginning of more to come.

9.   Repeat this cycle as often as needed for further transformation in other areas of your life. You will notice that the more you repeat, the more you receive and recognize abundance in your life.

In addition, The Seven Power Declarations may be recited during the 21 days or after the 21 days. These statements are designed to speak the power of abundance over and into your life.

The Prayer of Wisdom and Prayer of Thanks may be recited daily as a midday prayer. They may also be used to focus on obtaining wisdom or thanking God for manifestation.

Preparation

Before abundance can become a way of life, you must free yourself from the poverty mentality, ensure that you believe in abundance and be ready to receive even more. The truth is, lack, insufficiency and deficiency have hindered and possibly stopped the flow of abundance in your life. Poverty is an enemy of abundance and it needs to be dispelled from your mind forever. Just like you can't be hot and cold at the same time, you can't live in poverty and abundance at the same time. You must choose.

A poverty mentality comes from past experiences, family members or faulty mental thoughts about money. Saying "I never have enough" or "I'm always low on cash" are signs of a poverty mentality. Believing that piles and mounts of debt is a normal way of life has proven to be a poverty mentality. You were not designed to live from paycheck to paycheck. It is not a coincidence that you have THIS book in your hands, you can change your life by what you say and believe.

God's will is for you to have abundance. Abundance of all good things are God's ideas. He gave wealth and riches to Solomon when he asked for wisdom alone. Jesus died for you to have a better and more fulfilling life. You owe God an apology for not doing it His way, and for not believing in Him as your only source. How can you break free from your old ways of thinking and open up to God's best plan for you? Glad you asked.

I have included a special prayer of deliverance to help break the bondage of a poverty mentality and clear the path for abundance. God is ready to forgive you and change your life. Pray until you are fully free from your old way of thinking and know with all certainty that abundance is God ordained.

Prayer of Deliverance

Dear Lord,

How excellent You are in all the earth. I acknowledge that You have the ultimate plan for my present and future.

I ask that You forgive me for not seeking the truth in Your Word. Forgive me for believing the lie of lack as my portion. I have sinned against You and I repent for living a life of poverty, lack of prosperity and fear. I now put lack, insufficiency, fear, incompleteness, negativity, blame, deprivation, neediness, hardship, scarcity, shortage, inadequacy, deficiency, poorness, mediocrity, disobedience, lack of prosperity and sparsity on the cross of Jesus. Let the blood of Jesus cleanse my mind of all thoughts of poverty and lack. I renounce the power of a poverty mindset and its control over my life. I break the authority of all spirits that go contrary to the Word of God. I bind and cast out any spirit of the fear of wealth and abundance.

I now loose the spirit and promise of abundance into my life. I declare freedom from the grip of the enemy on my mind and my future as well as my well-being. I declare uncommon favor. I declare overflow of all things positive. I declare I will always have more than enough. I declare God's blessing and way of prosperity for my life. Grant me Your perfect and excellent way. Let me now receive your favor and blessings.

In Jesus Name I pray,
Amen

Kingdom Abundance Guidelines

Renewing your mind will pave the way for God's plan for your purpose in life. Below are basic guidelines for Kingdom abundance:

1.   You must practice Biblical Stewardship

Exodus 19:5
5 Now therefore, if ye will obey my voice indeed, and keep my covenant, then ye shall be a peculiar treasure unto me above all people: for all the earth is mine:
Job 41:11
11 Who hath prevented me, that I should repay him? whatsoever is under the whole heaven is mine.
Psalm 24:1
24 The earth is the LORD's, and the fulness thereof; the world, and they that dwell therein.

God owns everything. Whatever you have now, He gave it to you to take care of while it is in your possession. You don't own anything, but steward everything. You are an overseer of God's property. Therefore, you should make good use of all of your resources.

All of your money belongs to God. After the tithe and offerings, He is still interested in the 90% that's left. How you handle the 90% of your earnings is your opportunity to show God what a great steward you are over the rest of His money, an excellent overseer.   This means you are careful with how you spend the 90% of the money you have left. This means you make sure your obligations (needs) are met before spending money on other things you desire (wants). This means that you shouldn't use credit cards for purchases you can't afford.

God expects you to be productive and multiply the resources He has given to you and instead of spending all your money. You should seek out opportunities to increase money through investing, which means that a portion of your money should always be working for you.

When your stewardship pleases God, abundance flows. The formula is simple and works every time. The blessing of the Lord honors faithful stewards.

2.   Abundance is a heart thing

Luke 12:34
34 For where your treasure is, there will your heart be also.

What you care for, you take care of. You invest where your value is placed and where your heart is. Your attention is on what you love to do or who you love to be with. You spend your money where your heart is.

Your treasures are precious things of value and should be treated as such. Treasures such as money, jewels and coins are valuable to more than just you. A treasure can be exchanged for something you personally value.

When you exchange money for something you personally value, this is where your heart is attached. It is vital that your heart is in the right place. Show me where a person spends money and I will show you where their heart is. When God is your treasurer, He holds your treasure and your heart in place.

3.   Abundance is a faithful thing

Luke 16:11-12
11 If therefore ye have not been faithful in the unrighteous mammon, who will commit to your trust the true riches?
12 And if ye have not been faithful in that which is another man's, who shall give you that which is your own?

In this sense, being faithful is consistently doing the right thing with your abundance. When it comes to money, you know what is right, but may fail to do it. When you consistently do the right thing, you build trust with God. Consistent trust turns into trustworthiness. When you are trustworthy, more can be entrusted to you to grow, nurture, distribute and give as God leads or commands. You are the example others are watching. Thus, being faithful is a non-negotiable if you want abundance.

4.   Greed is NOT a part of Abundance

Proverbs 15:27
27 He that is greedy of gain troubleth his own house; but he that hateth gifts shall live.
Proverbs 28:22
22 He that hasteth to be rich hath an evil eye, and considereth not that poverty shall come upon him.
Proverbs 11:24-25
24 There is that scattereth, and yet increaseth; and there is that withholdeth more than is meet, but it tendeth to poverty.
25 The liberal soul shall be made fat: and he that watereth shall be watered also himself.

The Bible warns strongly against greed. Greed is also part of a poverty mindset. Our God is El Shaddai, the God who is more than enough. If you believe He is El Shaddai, there is no need to withhold His blessings. Withholding what can be used to help others, limits one's access to more abundance and can lead to poverty.

Giving is a prerequisite for the flow of abundance. First you give and in obedience to the process, you will be given back more than what you gave. Reaping what you sow is a law. You reap what you sow. You reap where you sow. Good or evil, you reap more than you sow.

5.   When wealth comes, follow God's instructions

Deuteronomy 8:11-18
11 Beware that thou forget not the LORD thy God, in not keeping his commandments, and his judgments, and his statutes, which I command thee this day:
12 Lest when thou hast eaten and art full, and hast built goodly houses, and dwelt therein;
13 And when thy herds and thy flocks multiply, and thy silver and thy gold is multiplied, and all that thou hast is multiplied;
14 Then thine heart be lifted up, and thou forget the LORD thy God, which brought thee forth out of the land of Egypt, from the house of bondage;
15 Who led thee through that great and terrible wilderness, wherein were fiery serpents, and scorpions, and drought, where there was no water; who brought thee forth water out of the rock of flint;
16 Who fed thee in the wilderness with manna, which thy fathers knew not, that he might humble thee, and that he might prove thee, to do thee good at thy latter end;
17 And thou say in thine heart, my power and the might of mine hand hath gotten me this wealth.
18 But thou shalt remember the LORD thy God: for it is he that giveth thee power to get wealth, that he may establish his covenant which he swore unto thy fathers, as it is this day.

1 Timothy 6:17-18
17 Charge them that are rich in this world, that they be not high-minded, nor trust in uncertain riches, but in the living God, who giveth us richly all things to enjoy;
18 That they do good, that they be rich in good works, ready to distribute, willing to communicate;

As wealthy people of God, you are responsible for your actions. You are on display. You must operate in integrity at all times and you must never take credit for what God has done.

This abundance journey is not about you at all. It is about the grace of God, the blessings of God and the wonders of God that you are about to manifest in your life. You do not put your trust in money, people or things. You trust only in the living God who gives you things to enjoy. As long as you keep this alignment correct, you will prosper by His will.

21 Abundance Affirmations

1. I boldly speak Abundance into my Life.
2. I move from a poverty mentality to believing in Abundance.
3. Money flows freely into my life.
4. I am happy to pay my bills on time, every time.
5. I am a cheerful giver.
6. I can be trusted with wealth and Abundance.
7. The more money I have access to, the more I am able to give and serve.
8. Money flows to me from expected and unexpected resources.
9. I am passionate about building wealth.
10. I accept and embrace wealth in my life because it is my portion.
11. My habits and behaviors create constant Prosperity.
12. Money expands my opportunities, experiences, options, choices and freedom.
13. I take full ownership over the management of my money.
14. I am prepared and will succeed.
15. Prosperity flows to me and through me.
16. I have access to resources that will positively impact my family, friends, community and region.
17. No thoughts, no setbacks, no delays shall steal my inheritance.
18. I am blessed in all walks of my life.
19. I am a good steward over God's resources.
20. I am thankful that provisions overflow in my life.
21. I receive fresh anointing for my purpose daily.

Morning Prayer

Father God,

Thank You that everything I need to fulfill my assignment has already been provided by Your will. I break any thoughts of lack and poverty that goes against Your will for my life. I declare that I live in the realm of unlimited possibilities and opportunities. Bring my words and actions in alignment with who You have called me to be and Your Kingdom agenda. I trust You to complete Your promises to me, and I stand in faith today believing Your Word shall come to pass in its season.

In the Name of Jesus I pray,
Amen

Evening Prayer

Father God,

You've proven Yourself faithful with another wonderful and fulfilled day. Let me now rest in Your Word and not my worries, with patience and belief. Renew my mind and give me a fresh anointing for the morning. Forgive me for any words spoken contrary to Your will. Download divine insights, revelations, creative ideas and concepts according to Your purpose for me. I trust You and believe You will grant me success with the work of my hands. I commit to walking in Your wisdom and blessings.

In the Name of Jesus I pray,
Amen.

Day 1   I boldly speak Abundance into my Life.

Having the right attitude and commitment to abundance is paramount and very necessary because the Word of God has proclaimed abundance for me. Abundance is available to me, so I speak and proclaim abundance into my life and I believe it will come. Because abundance is my birthright, I claim it with the words of my mouth. I am abundantly blessed. My speech is filled with words that welcome more than enough. I have what I need and more to give to others. I am thankful for what I have while seeking all that is readily available to me. I claim what is rightfully mine in Jesus name. When I speak, seek and believe, abundance comes. I cast out all thoughts of poverty or lack. I boldly speak abundance into my life.

Proverbs 18:21
21 Death and life are in the power of the tongue: and they that love it shall eat the fruit thereof.

Mark 11:23
23 For verily I say unto you, that whosoever shall say unto this mountain, Be thou removed, and be thou cast into the sea; and shall not doubt in his heart, but shall believe that those things which he saith shall come to pass; he shall have whatsoever he saith.

Psalm 122:7
7 Peace be within thy walls, and prosperity within thy palaces.

Day 2 I move from a poverty mentality to believing in Abundance.

I no longer believe the lie of poverty and lack. I do not lack anything nor cling to the chains of poverty. I am free and rid of poverty. Poverty has no place in my world and no control over my life. God's nature is to bless me a lot. He wants me to have every blessing He has promised me. I ask Him for my unique blessings and favor, the blessings that are meant for me. I live life more abundantly, up to the standard of abundance and not beneath God's will for me. I am excited that I am on the brink of abundance. My future days are greater than my past days. My territory is expanding. More is available to me when I truly believe beyond my current situation. I believe for better and greater. I want everything God has for me. I receive every gift God had prepared for me. I move from a poverty mentality to believing in Abundance.

1 Chronicles 4:10
10 And Jabez called on the God of Israel, saying, Oh! that thou wouldest bless me indeed, and enlarge my coast, and that thine hand might be with me, and that thou wouldest keep me from evil, that it may not grieve me! And God granted him that which he requested.

1 Timothy 6:17
17 Charge them that are rich in this world, that they be not high-minded, nor trust in uncertain riches, but in the living God, who giveth us richly all things to enjoy;

Day 3   Money flows freely into my life.

I now free any money that is mine to come to me. When I need money, I have it. I expect checks with my name on them in the mail every day. I receive dollars, coins and checks in my hand every time I need it. I have the money I need to meet my obligations. Money is not bound from me. I am blessed abundantly to be a blessing to others. God, make me a blessing to everyone around me as well as myself. I declare that My bank account is blessed. I declare that My investments are blessed and covered. I declare that My purse is blessed and there is money in my purse. I live under the kingdom system, not this earthly economy. My steps and financial decisions are ordered by the Lord. I make wise money moves. When I peel back the layers, I know it takes money to get things done. I do not toil for money to come my way. Money flows freely into my life.

Ecclesiastes 10:19
19 A feast is made for laughter, and wine maketh merry: but money answereth all things.

1 Kings 17:16
16 And the barrel of meal wasted not, neither did the cruse of oil fail, according to the word of the Lord, which he spake by Elijah.

Matthew 6:33
33 But seek ye first the kingdom of God, and his righteousness; and all these things shall be added unto you.

Day 4   I am happy to pay my bills on time, every time.

My bills are my obligations. When I purchase items on credit, I become accountable the moment I make the purchase. If I make bills, I owe for them. I am a person of integrity, and I cheerfully pay what I owe. I have enough to meet my responsibilities every month. I only create bills within my means and do not overspend. I master my money and assign each dollar a task. I know the amount of my monthly bills and live within my financial boundaries and capabilities. I pay my bills stress free. I make smart decisions with my purchases. I work to pay everything off, so I will not owe anyone anything but love and offer help to people. I am happy to pay my bills on time, every time.

Romans 13:8
8 Owe no man anything, but to love one another: for he that loveth another hath fulfilled the law.

Ecclesiastes 5:5
5 Better is it that thou shouldest not vow, than that thou shouldest vow and not pay.

Psalm 37:21
21 The wicked borroweth, and payeth not again: but the righteous sheweth mercy, and giveth.

Day 5   I am a cheerful giver.

God loves a cheerful giver. He first gave to me, so I can give to others. When I give cheerfully, I show the characteristics of my Father. God smiles when I give cheerfully. I give to make room for more. I give out of abundance and sufficiency, so I always have enough left when I give. God has allowed me another day to share His goodness and mercy with someone else. I will look for someone to bless today with my gifts. I will give a smile and a kind word. Someone is relying on me to give. Giving is not a burden, but my pleasure. As I have seed to sow, I reap the benefits of my seed. I am a cheerful giver.

2 Corinthians 9:7
7 Every man according to his purpose in his heart, so let him give; not grudgingly, or of necessity: for God loveth a cheerful giver.

Luke 6:38
38 Give, and it shall be given unto you; good measure, pressed down, shaken together, and running over, shall men give into your bosom. For with the same measure that ye mete withal it shall be measured to you again.

Acts 20:35
35 I have shewed you all things, how that so laboring ye ought to support the weak, and to remember the words of the Lord Jesus, how he said, it is more blessed to give than to receive.

Day 6   I can be trusted with wealth and Abundance.

Abundance is overflow. I have a large amount in which I have been trusted. Everything I have God gave me. I use my resources wisely. God has trusted me with little and given me a lot. My resources work together for my own good. I am confident that I can take care of my wealth and abundance. I am a caretaker of the resources God has entrusted to me. My investments grow. My little grows into much. My bank account has more than enough. I make sound decisions with money and I am rewarded with more when I value what I already have. I can be trusted with wealth and Abundance.

Luke 12:48
48 But he that knewth not, and didth commit things worthy of stripes, shall be beaten with few stripes. For unto whomsoever much is given, of him shall be much required: and to whom men hath committed much, of him they will ask the more.

1 Corinthians 4:2
2 Moreover it is required in stewards, that a man be found faithful.

Luke 16:10
10 He that is faithful in that which is least is faithful also in much: and he that is unjust in the least is unjust also in much.

Day 7   The more money I have access to, the more I am able to give and serve.

As I increase, my family increases, my friends increase, my service increases and my charitable giving increases. People around me are blessed through my free will giving. I am blessed to be a blessing to others. My access is to my money and the money of others. My debt is decreasing. My spending is personal, but the effects are public. My spending is a public show of personal intentions. My good deeds are magnified and are a reflection of blessings from God. I sow in good ground and reap a bountiful harvest therein. I am careful where I sow and where I plant. I am a giver. The more money I have access to, the more I am able to give and serve.

Proverbs 22:9
9 He that hath a bountiful eye shall be blessed; for he giveth of his bread to the poor.

2 Corinthians 9:10
10 Now he that ministereth seed to the sower both ministers bread for your food, and multiply your seed sown, and increase the fruits of your righteousness.

Deuteronomy 15:10
10 Thou shalt surely give him, and thine heart shall not be grieved when thou givest unto him: because that for this thing the Lord thy God shall bless thee in all thy works, and in all that thou puttest thine hand unto.

Day 8   Money flows to me from expected and unexpected resources.

God is my source, my provider and my protector. I depend on Him for everything. God puts me on the mind and hearts of others to bless me. Money comes from unusual places. I receive checks in the mail on a regular basis. I am favored by others and I get quality discounts, gifts, inheritances, job promotions, bonuses, increases, contracts, greener opportunities and new clients. My job is only one of my resources of abundance in wealth. I am grateful for a steady influx of money. I have ridiculous favor on my life, expect great things and am not surprised when doors open. Money flows to me from expected and unexpected resources.

Deuteronomy 8:18
18 But thou shalt remember the Lord thy God: for it is he that giveth thee power to get wealth, that he may establish his covenant which he sware unto thy fathers, as it is this day.

Joshua 1:8
8 This book of the law shall not depart out of thy mouth; but thou shalt meditate therein day and night, that thou mayest observe to do according to all that is written therein: for then thou shalt make thy way prosperous, and then thou shalt have good success.

Day 9   I am passionate about building wealth.

My money works for me. It is good for my money to grow. My wealth increases as my investments prosper, time after time. I do not just trade time for money. The Lord has given me a mind to create and strengthened my body to produce. I am blessed in my purse. I am blessed in my bank. My income is blessed. My outgo is blessed and my giving is blessed. I am excited to see the works of my hands provide for my family and future. I will leave an inheritance to my descendants. Building wealth is a blessing not a grind. I am passionate about building wealth.

Proverbs 13:22
22 A good man leaveth an inheritance to his children's children: and the wealth of the sinner is laid up for the just.

Proverbs 28:19
19 He that tilleth his land shall have plenty of bread: but he that followeth after vain persons shall have poverty enough.

Proverbs 10:4
4 He becometh poor that dealeth with a slack hand: but the hand of diligent maketh rich.

Day 10 I accept and embrace wealth in my life because it is my portion.

I put the past behind me and welcome wealth abundantly. My mind and heart are open to wealth. My health is good, and I have more than enough money to meet my needs and the needs of others. The poor will be with us, so I raise my hand to meet their needs and help them. I desire a blessed life. God adds wealth to me with no sorry. Through the finished work of Jesus on the cross, I have salvation, health and prosperity. Wealth and riches are in my house, and I hold onto what is rightfully mine. My Father is rich and I lack nothing. I accept and embrace wealth in my life because it is my portion.

Psalm: 112:3
3 Wealth and riches shall be in his house: and his righteousness endureth for ever.

Ecclesiastes 5:18-19
18 Behold that which I have seen: it is good and comely for one to eat and drink, and to enjoy the good of all his labour that he taketh under the sun all the days of his life, which God giveth him: for it is his portion.
19 Every man also to whom God hath given riches and wealth, and hath given him power to eat thereof, and to take his portion, and to rejoice in his labour; this is the gift of God.

Deuteronomy 7:13

13 And he will love thee, and bless thee, and multiply thee: he will also bless the fruit of thy womb, and the fruit of thy land, thy corn, and thy wine and thine oil, the increase of thy kine, and the flocks of thy sheep, in the land which he sware unto thy fathers to give thee.

Day 11   My habits and behaviors create constant Prosperity.

My work ethic causes me to prosper. I work as I am working unto God. I do my work with excellence. I am the best at the work I do. I represent the Kingdom of God with my work ethic. My faith in action causes me to prosper. My plans and goals are a part of my prosperity plan. God blesses my determination and consistency. Prosperity flows easily because of my actions. I follow wise council to prosper. I prosper as my soul prospers. On a scale of poverty and prosperity, I win with absolute prosperity. I count the costs before purchasing large items. My savings accounts are blessed. I earn money and my money works for me. My habits and behaviors create constant Prosperity.

Galatians: 6:9
9 And let us not be weary in well doing: for in due season we shall reap, if we faint not.

2 Thessalonians 3:10
10 For even when we were with you, this we commanded you, that if any would not work, neither should he eat.

Psalm 118:25
25 Save now, I beseech thee, O Lord: O Lord, I beseech thee, send now prosperity.

Job 42:10
10 And the Lord turned the captivity of Job, when he prayed for his friends: also the Lord gave Job twice as much as he had before.

Day 12   Money expands my opportunities, experiences, options, choices and freedom.

As my money grows, I experience new opportunities. The more money I have, the more I can choose. I can choose to learn more, to better my situation, to invest, to help others and to expand my reach. I can choose my retirement date. I can choose my retirement amount. More money gives me more options. I can give without fear of running out. I can help more people. Money affords me the freedom to purchase at will, live to certain standards, give liberally and be in control of my time. My money affords me the ability to enjoy life and to donate to help the lives of others. Money expands my opportunities, experiences, options, choices and freedom.

Exodus 1:7
7 And the children of Israel were fruitful, and increased abundantly, and multiplied, and waxed exceedingly mighty; and the land was filled with them.

Psalm 145:16
16 Thou openest thine hand, and satisfies the desire of every living thing.

Day 13   I take full ownership over the management of my money.

I have caught the vision and my money management is non-negotiable. My vision is my validated victory. I know my monthly and annual financial goals, and my vision is clear. I own my financial responsibilities and meet them. I have victory over poverty and lack. My money moves are decent and in order. I have tabulated how much I make and how much I spend. I must respect how much I spend, save and give. I pay close attention to my spending and savings habits. I must invest wisely and without fear, so that my money grows. I ask God for insight to my investments, and I follow His directions. Because I am a good money manager, God blesses the increase. I take full ownership over the management of my money.

Genesis 2:4-5
4 These are the generations of the heavens and of the earth when they were created, in the day that the Lord God made the earth and the heavens,
5 And every plant of the field before it was in the earth, and every herb of the field before it grew: for the Lord God had not caused it to rain upon the earth, and there was not a man to till the ground.

Luke 14:28
28 For which of you, intending to build a tower, sitteth not down first, and counteth the cost, whether he have sufficient to finish it?

Day 14   I am prepared and will succeed.

I have studied and continue to learn about money management and investments. When preparation meets opportunity, success occurs. As I put principles into action, I will see results. I follow the patterns that create wealth. I learn and develop money strategies. Once I know my money strategies and the data recalculates, my pace to my financial destiny changes. Once my pace changes, my time of arrival to my financial destination is faster. I plant seeds to multiply and God gives the increase. I work during planting season and reap during harvest season. I am prepared and will succeed.

Job 28:27
27 Then did he see it, and declare it; he prepared it, yea, and searched it out.

Proverbs 24:27
27 Prepare thy work without, and make it fit for thyself in the field; and afterwards build thine house.

Day 15   Prosperity flows to me and through me.

I humble myself to the will and way of God. I can be trusted to distribute resources to the poor and needy. God knows me. God knows my intentions and my heart. He sees my will and my works. My ways are magnified as I receive increase. God will grant me success so I can bless others. I accept God's partnership to impact others. I give from my overflow. My cup runs over. I do my part to impact the world. The work I do for the Kingdom is not about me, but all about God. I have more than enough to share with others. I am willing to expand from where I am to where God wants me to be. Prosperity flows to me and through me.

Deuteronomy 16:17
17 Every man shall give as he is able, according to the blessing of the Lord thy God which he hath given thee.

2 Corinthians 9:8
8 And God is able to make all grace abound toward you; that you, always having all sufficiency in all things, may abound to every good work:

Day 16   I have access to resources that will positively impact my family, friends, community and region.

My current resources are only a portion of what I have available to me. I am abundantly blessed with time, talents, ideas and connections. All the resources I am blessed with are at God's disposal. I am the solution to someone's problem. Unless I complete my assignment, it will not be completed. As I gain more resources, I will look beyond my current assignment. My impact on others is supplied directly by God. I will positively impact my church, community, workplace and territory. As God causes men to give to me, I respond to my family's wants and needs. As resources pour into me, my portion to give is expanded. I am thankful that God has chosen me to help His people. I have access to resources that will positively impact my family, friends, community and region.

Ephesians 2:10
10 For we are His workmanship, created in Christ Jesus for good works, which God prepared beforehand that we should walk in them.

Malachi 3:10
10 Bring ye all the tithes into the storehouse, that there may be meat in mine house, and prove me now herewith, saith the Lord of hosts, if I will not open you the windows of heaven, and pour you out a blessing, that there shall not be room enough to receive it.

Psalm 115:14

14 The Lord shall increase you more and more, you and your children.

Day 17   No thoughts, no setbacks, no delays shall steal my inheritance.

My inheritance is defined by the Old and New Testament which has been willed to me by my Heavenly Father. I relinquish any negative thoughts that will hold me back. I now cancel all setbacks and delays. I let go of every hindering relationship and remove myself from negativity. I ask God to sharpen my discernment. I don't waste time trying to please people not in alignment with my financial future. By God's grace, no curse shall steal my inheritance. I declare I will receive all that is mine. My dreams will be accomplished. No weapon formed against me shall prosper. I am a beneficiary in line for what is rightfully mine. What the enemy meant for evil, God turned it around for good. I am elevated to a different level because I survived the test. No thoughts, no setbacks, no delays shall steal my inheritance.

Isaiah 54:17
17 No weapon formed against thee shall prosper; and every tongue that shall rise against thee in judgment thou shall condemn. This is the heritage of the servants of the Lord, and their righteousness is of me, saith the Lord.

Proverbs 3:9-10
9 Honour the Lord with thy substance, and with the first fruits of all thine increase:
10 So shall thy barns be filled with plenty, and thy presses shall burst out with new wine.

2 Chronicles 26:5

5 And he sought God in the days of Zechariah, who had understanding in the visions of God: and as long as he sought the Lord, God made him to prosper.

Day 18   I am blessed in all walks of my life.

Because God is the head of my life, my leader and my protector, I follow Him. He is my source and provider. I prosper as my soul prospers. I am blessed when I enter my home and when I leave my home. Clients are looking to do business with me. I show up on assignment. I am blessed in my finances, family and relationships. My friendships and business relationships flourish. People want to connect with me. I am in the right place at the right time to be blessed. What the enemy sends to harm me, God turns it around for good. I am blessed in my body. I cancel any illnesses and call my body to function as God has designed. My home and car are covered by the blood of Jesus. God has divine connections prepared for my arrival. I lack nothing, but have more than enough. I am blessed in all walks of my life.

Psalm 37:4
4 Delight thyself also in the Lord, and he shall give thee the desires of thine heart.

Psalm 1:3
3 And he shall be like a tree planted by the rivers of water, that bringeth forth his fruit in his season; his leaf also shall not wither; and whatsoever he doeth shall prosper.

Day 19   I am a good steward over God's resources.

Everything I have God gave me. He trusts me with His property. I will care for my job, my house, my car, my family, my friends, my talents and my money. He has entrusted precious things in my hands and I will take care of them wholeheartedly. I oversee money, people and things for the King. I am grateful for the responsibility He has given me. I impact others as a good steward. What I do with what I have determines God's next move for me. Success is a product of what I do with what I have. I work for God, not myself. I will be held accountable for how I handle God's property. I am a good steward over God's resources.

Matthew 25:14-30
14 "For the kingdom of heaven is like a man travelling into a far country, who called his own servants, and delivered unto them his goods. 15 And unto one he gave five talents, to another two, and to another one, to every man according to his several ability; and straightway took his journey. 16 Then he that had received the five talents went and traded with the same, and made them other five talents. 17 And likewise he that had received two, he also gained other two. 18 But he that had received one went and digged in the earth, and hid his lord's money. 19 After a long time the lord of those servants cometh, and reckoneth with them

20 And so he who had received five talents came and brought five other talents, saying, Lord, thou deliveredst unto me five talents: behold, I have gained besides them five talents more. 21 His lord said to him, 'Well done, thou good and faithful servant; thou has been faithful over a few things, I will make thee ruler over many things: enter thou into the joy of thy lord.' 22 He also that had received two talents came and said, 'Lord, you deliveredst unto me two talents: behold, I have gained two other talents besides them.' 23 His lord said to him, Well done, good and faithful servant; thou hast been faithful over a few things, I will make thee ruler over many things: enter into the joy of thy lord.

24 Then he which had received the one talent came and said, 'Lord, I knew thee that thou art an hard man, reaping where thou hast not sown, and gathering where thou hast not strawed: 25 And I was afraid, and went and hid thy talent in the earth: lo, there thou hast that is thine.'

26 "His lord answered and said to him, 'Thou wicked and slothful servant, thou knewest that I reap where I sow not, and gather where I have not strawed: 27 Thou oughtest therefore to have put my money to the exchangers, and then at my coming I should have received mine own with usury. 28 Take therefore the talent from him, and give it unto him which hath ten talents.

29 For unto every one that hath shall be given, and he shall have abundance: but from him that hath not shall be taken away even that which he hath. 30 And cast ye the unprofitable servant into outer darkness: there shall be weeping and gnashing of teeth.

Day 20   I am thankful that provisions overflow in my life.

God has provided me with everything I need to succeed. When I need something, it is provided. I embrace a life of overflow like Solomon, David and Abraham. I have the capacity to start and finish a thing. I am thankful for my overflow. My daily provisions and blessings overflow. My portion is an overflowing cup. I am a lender and not a borrower. I declare that God provides me with all I will ever need. I am thankful to God, my Provider. I am thankful that provisions overflow in my life.

Psalm 84:11
11 For the Lord God is a sun and shield: the Lord will give grace and glory: no good thing will He withhold from them that walk uprightly.

Psalm 23:5
5 Thou preparest a table before me in the presence of mine enemies: thou anointest my head with oil; my cup runneth over.

2 Chronicles 32: 27-29
27 And Hezekiah had exceeding much riches and honour: and he made himself treasuries for silver, and for gold, and for precious stones, and for spices, and for shields, and for all manner of pleasant jewels;
28 Storehouses also for the increase of corn, and wine, and oil; and stalls for all manner of beasts, and cotes for flocks.

29 Moreover he provided him cities, and possessions of flocks and herds in abundance: for God had given him substance very much.

2 Corinthians 9:11-12

11 Being enriched in everything to all bountifulness, which causeth through us thanksgiving to God.

12 For the administration of this service not only supplieth the want of the saints, but is abundant also by many thanksgivings unto God

Day 21   I receive fresh anointing for my purpose daily.

I rely on God for everything and ask Him to give me what I need daily. He knows the power I will need over my tongue today. Each day is different and He knows me better than I know myself. Each day has new mercies and my spirit is renewed. My mind is clear for what God has for me today. I am greeted with goodness, and I rejoice. I wake up to thankfulness, and I am happy. Yesterday is done and I have another chance to get it right. I have daily bread for my daily strength. I relish in each moment of life with love. I cherish each breath I am given. I pause for new instructions from my Father. God crowns my head with knowledge. I receive fresh anointing for my purpose daily.

Exodus 31:11
11 And the anointing oil, and sweet incense for the holy place: according to all that I have commanded thee shall they do.

Psalm 118:24
24 This is the day which the Lord hath made; we will rejoice and be glad in it.

Psalm 68:19
19 Blessed be the Lord, who daily loadeth us with benefits, even the God of our salvation. Selah

Seven Power Declarations

(May be used during or after 21 days for encouragement)

Holy Spirit, give me fresh revelation daily.

The Blessing of God covers me and my family.

Divine connections are headed my way.

Today is my best day and better days are ahead.

I have a flood of opportunities and options waiting on me.

I attract avalanches of Favor to me and those attached to me.

God delights in my successes and has a perfect master plan.

Prayer of Wisdom

Father God,

As I grow in my assignment, grant me wisdom and understanding according to your Word. You are the all-knowing God. You know everything, you see everything and you hear everything. You are omniscient. You love me enough to know the number of hairs on my head, so I trust You. I humbly ask for You to give me wisdom, make me wise in speech and wise in relationships. Give me wisdom for business. Give me insight and sensitivity for Your direction in my life. Make me wise in my finances. Sharpen my discernment for making decisions. I accept your direction, and I desire to do life Your way. Be merciful with my mistakes and forgive me for ignoring Your help in the past. I believe You have plans for me to prosper and to give me hope and a future. Let Your wisdom reign down on me. My God, grant me wisdom and understanding.

In Jesus Name
Amen

Proverbs 9:10
10 The fear of the Lord is the beginning of wisdom: and the knowledge of the holy is understanding.

2 Chronicles 1:10-12
10 Give me now wisdom and knowledge, that I may go out and come in before this people: for who can judge this thy people, that is so great?

11 And God said to Solomon, Because this was in thine heart, and thou hast not asked riches, wealth, or honour, nor the life of thine enemies, neither yet hast asked long life; but hast asked wisdom and knowledge for thyself, that thou mayest judge my people, over whom I have made thee king:

12 Wisdom and knowledge is granted unto thee; and I will give thee riches, and wealth, and honour, such as none of the kings have had that have been before thee, neither shall there any after thee have the like.

Prayer of Thanks

Dear Lord,

I love You, I adore You and I am grateful to You. I am humbled to be in your presence. You are Lord over my life and without You I am nothing. I bless You and praise your Holy Name. I thank You for life, health and strength. You have saved me from Hell, and I want to say Thank You. Thank You for caring enough to correct me when I do wrong and comfort me when I am sad. Everything I have comes from You. You are my protector and my provider. Thank You for keeping me from evil and the devouring enemy. Thank You so much for giving your Son, Jesus Christ, to die for our sins and iniquities. Thank You for friends and family as I pray for the abandoned and lonely. You have renewed my mind and increased my faith. I thank You for your faithfulness, mercy and goodness. You are a good, good Father, and the manifestation of your goodness is prevalent in my life. Thank You most of all for the unfailing love and care You have continued to give in spite of me. I love You. I adore You and I thank You.

In Jesus Name I pray,
Amen

1 Thessalonians 5:18
18 In everything give thanks; for this is the will of God in Christ Jesus concerning you.

Philippians 4:6
6 Be careful for nothing; but in everything by prayer and supplication with thanksgiving let your requests be made known unto God.

1 Chronicles 16:34
34 O give thanks unto the Lord; for he is good: for his mercy endureth for ever.

Psalm 100:4
4 Enter into his gates with thanksgiving, and into his courts with praise: be thankful unto him, and bless his name.

Colossians 3:15
15 And let the peace of Christ rule in your hearts, to the which also ye are called in one body; and be ye thankful.

Ephesians 5:20
20 Giving thanks always for all things unto God and the Father in the name of our Lord Jesus Christ;

Psalms 136:1-3
1 O give thanks unto the Lord; for his is good: for his mercy endureth for ever.
2 O give thanks unto the God of gods: for his mercy endureth for ever.
3 O give thanks to the Lord of lords: for his mercy endureth for ever.

Conclusion

13 Because of this act of ministry, [a]they will glorify God for your obedience to the gospel of Christ which you confess, as well as for your generous participation [in this gift] for them and for all [the other believers in need], 14 and they also long for you while they pray on your behalf, because of the surpassing measure of God's grace [His undeserved favor, mercy, and blessing which is revealed] in you. 15 Now thanks be to God for His indescribable gift [which is precious beyond words]!

2 Corinthians 9:13-15(AMP)

Bless You ALL!
Adrienne Earls,
"Master Money Mogul"

About the Author

Adrienne Earls is an author, money coach, landlord, Realtor and corporate manager. Her mission is to transform individuals into money masters. Adrienne addresses critical money issues affecting the social economical and spiritual insight of women all over the world.

Adrienne is the owner of Signature Money Systems and has earned the title "Master Money Mogul" on social media platforms. She has a Business Administration degree from Southwestern University and several insurance and real estate designations including a Chartered Financial Consultant. Adrienne is also the official photographer for the National Primitive Baptist Convention, USA.

In her spare time, Adrienne enjoys spending time with family and close friends. When she's not studying her craft, she can be caught flying her drone or playing the bass guitar.

www.ingramcontent.com/pod-product-compliance
Lightning Source LLC
Chambersburg PA
CBHW071102090426

42737CB00013B/2434